Avionics:
Instruments and Auxiliary Systems
Vision, Threat Avoidance, Bench, Emergency

Student Workbook

Production Staff

Designer/Photographer Dustin Blyer
Senior Designer/Production Manager Roberta Byerly
Contributor David Jones
Editor Jeff Strong

© Copyright 2017 by
Avotek Information Resources, LLC.
All Rights Reserved

International Standard Book Number 1-933189-58-4
ISBN 13: 978-1-933189-58-1
Order # T-AVINAU-0102

For Sale by: Avotek
A Select Aerospace Industries, Inc., company

Mail to:
P.O. Box 219
Weyers Cave, VA 24486
USA

Ship to:
200 Packaging Drive
Weyers Cave, VA 24486
USA

Toll Free: 800-828-6835
Telephone: 540-234-9090
Fax: 540-234-9399

First Edition
Second Printing
Printed in the USA

www.avotek.com

Contents

To the Student — iv

1 Aircraft Instruments — 1

2 Radar Systems — 15

3 Air Traffic Surveillance and Warning — 23

4 Weather and Terrain Awareness and Avoidance — 33

5 Synthetic and Enhanced Vision — 39

6 Avionics Bench Equipment and Practices — 45

7 Emergency-Related Avionics — 53

To the Student

This student workbook accompanies *Avionics: Instruments and Auxiliary Systems*, which is part of the avionics series created and published by Avotek. This workbook should be used as a tool for highlighting the strengths, and pinpointing the weaknesses, of the avionics student gathering the skill and knowledge necessary to build a strong foundation in the avionics field. Specifically, it evaluates progress made in subject areas.

In writing this workbook, Avotek used the principle that the student is actively engaged in obtaining the skills and knowledge necessary to function well as a technician in the avionics field. Questions on each chapter of the text are divided into three question formats and printed on perforated sheets for removal and presentation.

Fill in the Blank
These questions are designed to help the student understand new terminology and fundamental facts essential to understanding the chapter material.

Multiple Choice
These questions offer a broader overview of the material by offering several possible answers and allowing the student to identify the correct answer, either through recognition or through the process of elimination.

Analysis
These are complex questions that require the student to access information presented in the text, analyze the data, and record a response. Successful completion of the analysis questions shows the student has a thorough understanding of the material presented in the chapter.

The answers for each set of questions are available from your course instructor.

Avotek® Aircraft Maintenance Series
Introduction to Aircraft Maintenance
Aircraft Structural Maintenance
Aircraft System Maintenance
Aircraft Powerplant Maintenance

Avotek Aircraft Avionics Series
Avionics: Fundamentals of Aircraft Electronics
Avionics: Beyond the AET
Avionics: Instruments and Auxiliary Systems
Avionics: Systems and Troubleshooting

Other Books by Avotek
Advanced Composites
Aircraft Corrosion Control Guide
Aircraft Hydraulics
Aircraft Structural Technician
Aircraft Turbine Engines
Aircraft Wiring & Electrical Installation
AMT Reference Handbook
Avotek Aeronautical Dictionary
Fundamentals of Modern Aviation
Light Sport Aircraft Inspection Procedures
Structural Composites: Advanced Composites in Aviation
Transport Category Aircraft Systems

Chapter 1
Aircraft Instruments

FILL IN THE BLANK QUESTIONS

name:

date:

1. The _____ was an early instrument that allowed pilots to fly level in conditions that prevented pilots from seeing land.

2. The _____ and the _____ are electronics that became a vital part of instruments' operation and construction.

3. Modern instrument information is displayed on a/an _____ rather than on the original analog gauge.

4. Most modern instruments have two parts: the _____ and the _____ .

5. Varying electrical resistance in a circuit can be used in instruments to indicate _____ , _____ , or _____ .

6. A clear tube or panel connected to a tank or reservoir that allows the pilot to see the fluid level in the tank is an example of a/an _____ .

7. The _____ is the term describing a modern flight deck consisting primarily of digital computer displays.

8. The display between the pilots and the front windshield is called the _____ _____ .

9. A synchro, used to indicate the position or condition of a component that is remote from the flight deck, has two main components: _____ and _____ .

10. A differential synchro measures two _____ .

11. Instruments send readings and information in _____ through a digital data bus and to the aircraft's central computer.

12. An aircraft's basic pitot-static system has three indicators: _____ , _____ , and _____ .

13. As aircraft approach the _____ , impact and static pressure dynamics change, rendering a basic pitot-static system inaccurate.

14. A/An _____ is a model of the atmosphere at MSL with pressure of 29.92 inches of mercury, which is equal to 14.70 pounds per square inch, and temperature of 59°F (15°C).

15. The _____ bounces a wave off the ground and measures the time it takes to return to the aircraft to determine the distance above ground level.

16. The _____ is a system that compensates for altitude and other pitot-static errors so the flight crew has accurate altitude, airspeed, and vertical speed readings.

Chapter 1
Aircraft Instruments

FILL IN THE BLANK QUESTIONS

name:

date:

17. Changes in airflow cause the internal or external _____ to rotate, thus detecting the angle of attack.

18. Some aircraft angle of attack systems have a/an _____ to alert the pilot if the aircraft is approaching a stall because of the combinations of angle of attack, flaps position, and slats position.

19. Digital pressure sensors in a solid-state pressure sensor rely on the _____, which uses crystalline materials such as quartz disks that generate electrical signals when under pressure.

20. A/An _____ turns on to indicate when the aircraft is within 1,000 ft. of a preselected, target altitude.

21. A gyroscope can have different _____, depending on how many gimbals support the gyroscope and their arrangement.

22. The gyroscope in a turn-and-bank indicator responds only to motion around the _____ axis and is not affected by rolling or pitching.

23. Most modern jet aircraft use the _____ as the primary gyroscope reference system.

24. Standby instruments serving as a backup if a computer or electrical failure occurs typically includes the following configuration: _____, _____, and _____.

25. The _____ shows the load on the aircraft structure in gravitation (g) units.

26. The tachometer indicates a reciprocating engine's _____ and a turbine engine's compressor section as the _____.

27. Measuring fuel flow accurately is complicated because fuel mass changes with _____ or with the _____ used in turbine engines.

28. In oil temperature sensor systems, two types use a/an _____ oil thermometer and a third uses a/an _____ to measure the oil vapor's expansion properties, which are associated with the temperature.

29. Because multiengine aircraft operate more smoothly when the engines run at the same speed, they are equipped with _____ and _____.

30. _____ and _____, which is an alloy of copper and nickel, are used in thermocouples to measure exhaust gas temperatures.

Chapter 1
Aircraft Instruments

FILL IN THE BLANK QUESTIONS

name:

date:

31. In reciprocating engines, gasket thermocouples are placed under the spark plug and used to measure the temperature at the _____.

32. The pressure indicator for the engine's intake is used to manage _____ in relation to fuel flow and propeller pitch and to achieve various performance profiles in different phases of run-up and flight.

33. Pressure-sensing pitot-type probes used at a turbine engine's inlet and outlet are measured and used to calculate the _____, which represents thrust.

34. _____ and _____ are two systems that monitor aircraft systems and conditions and inform the flight crew of the engine statuses and warnings via two monitors.

35. In large aircraft in which the flight crew cannot see the wing flaps, the _____ displays the situation.

36. Modern aircraft commonly use a hydraulic system pressure of _____ p.s.i.

37. Although advanced navigation tools are available, one navigational aid system, the _____ system, has been in service since the World War II era and is still used.

38. _____ and _____ also integrate VOR information to automatically control the aircraft on its planned flight segments.

39. An instrument landing system broadcasts signals from two antenna systems, the _____ and _____, to guide aircraft to a safe landing on the runway.

40. Marker beacons' transmissions are very narrow and are directed _____.

41. The _____ combines indications from a magnetic compass, VOR, and automatic direction finder (ADF) in one instrument to always show the magnetic heading.

42. The global positioning system (GPS) uses 21 satellites to provide worldwide location coordinates by _____ reference rather than in relation to ground-based stations.

43. An aircraft receiver uses three satellites' location transmission to determine exact position. By incorporating the distance to a fourth satellite, the unit can calculate the aircraft's _____.

Chapter 1
Aircraft Instruments

FILL IN THE BLANK QUESTIONS

name:

date:

44. In most electronic flight information systems (EFIS), each pilot has two panels—one typically displaying attitude and heading information (such as the EHSI), the other displaying _____ .

45. After the flight crew enters the route and performance data for the flight and the flight is underway, the flight director indicator (FDI) provides the _____ .

46. The electronic horizontal situation indicator's (EHSI) _____ shows the aircraft against a detailed moving map background along with navigational aids, other airports, and waypoints.

47. Instrument gauge markings indicate the following: _____ is the normal operating range, _____ is a caution range, and _____ is a dangerous operation range that is not to be exceeded.

48. To absorb low-frequency, high-amplitude shocks, instrument panels are mounted with sets of square-plated absorbers called _____ .

49. On multiengine aircraft, compare the instruments for the engines. Any _____ can indicate a faulty engine, component, or instrument.

50. When troubleshooting faulty instruments, the first step is a/an _____ . Look for discolored or burned wires and terminal boards, corroded switch contacts, broken or frayed wires, loose connector plugs, and loose _____ .

51. Maintaining pitot tubes can be dangerous because they are _____ . To properly test one, monitor the _____ when turning it on.

Chapter 1
Aircraft Instruments

MULTIPLE CHOICE QUESTIONS

name:

date:

1. The six instruments in the traditional six pack are
   a. Altimeter, airspeed indicator, radio magnetic indicator, vertical speed indicator, artificial horizon, directional gyro/heading indicator
   b. Airspeed indicator, artificial horizon/attitude indicator, altimeter, turn and bank indicator, directional gyro/heading indicator, vertical speed indicator
   c. Engine speed indicator, airspeed indicator, turn and bank indicator, vertical speed indicator, artificial horizon, directional gyro/heading indicator
   d. Altimeter, angle of attack indicator, turn and bank indicator, vertical speed indicator, artificial horizon, radio magnetic indicator

2. Modern aircraft use what to monitor instruments for problems, relieving pilots from needing to constantly monitor them?
   a. Computers
   b. High-lo gauges
   c. Sight gauges
   d. Air data charts

3. Sensors that detect the position of aircraft components such as stabilizers, rudder, flaps, slats and others, use what electrical components?
   a. Resistance diodes and potentiometers
   b. Variable transformers and transistors
   c. Variable resistors and wheatstone bridges
   d. Variable resistors and potentiometers

4. An instrument with a dial marked with a range along which the needle moves radially to point at the appropriate measurement on the range best describes what kind of instrument?
   a. Vertical scale instrument
   b. Conventional analog instrument
   c. Digital display instrument
   d. Sight gauge

5. In torque indicating synchros, the stator windings are how many degrees apart?
   a. 60°
   b. 90°
   c. 120°
   d. 180°

6. One of the digital data buses' benefits over older, analog systems connecting transmitters to the indicators in the cockpit is what?
   a. Less weight
   b. No wires
   c. No redundant backups are needed
   d. All the above

7. The hole at the tip of the pitot tube is used to detect what kind of pressure?
   a. Blunt pressure
   b. Total pressure
   c. Ambient pressure
   d. Normal, atmospheric pressure

8. Static air ports are mounted on what parts of the aircraft?
   a. Trailing edge of the wings
   b. Leading edge of the wings
   c. Side of the fuselage
   d. Tip of the aircraft nose

9. The airspeed indicator measures the difference between what two pressures to calculate the airspeed?
   a. Impact pressure and static pressure
   b. Pressure on one side of the fuselage and pressure on the other side
   c. Total pressure and impact pressure
   d. Diaphragm pressure and impact pressure

10. The speed of sound (called Mach) at sea level at _____ degrees Fahrenheit is _____ knots.
    a. 59°, 661 knots
    b. 30°, 643 knots
    c. –41°, 594 knots
    d. All the above

11. To manually calculate altitude above ground level, subtract the elevation of the terrain beneath the aircraft (referenced on the charts) from the altitude displayed on the altimeter. Another instrument that gives this without the need for manual calculation is what?
    a. Absolute altimeter
    b. Servo altimeter
    c. Radar altimeter
    d. Analog altimeter

Chapter 1
Aircraft Instruments

MULTIPLE CHOICE QUESTIONS

name:

date:

12. Above 18,000 ft., all altimeters are set to 29.92 (pressure altitude) so that all aircraft use the same barometric pressure setting and, therefore, can operate safely with the proper what?
    a. Latitude and longitude
    b. Vertical separation
    c. Horizontal and vertical altitude
    d. Horizontal separation

13. Some modern aircraft do not have a unit called the digital air data computer. Instead, what unit calculates all functions and calculations of an air data computer using information it receives as signals over a data bus?
    a. Radar altimeter
    b. Central computing system
    c. Angle of attack computer
    d. Vertical speed indicator

14. The static air temperature plus any temperature increase caused by air friction on the aircraft flying at high speeds is called what?
    a. Mach temperature
    b. Ambient temperature
    c. Ram temperature
    d. Total air temperature

15. Before digital computers, pilots used a type of analog computer or disc calculator, such as a Felsenthal PT computer, Aero Products Research CR-6 (Aviation) Computer, or a Dalton type Dead Reckoning Computer E6-B, to calculate what?
    a. Groundspeed only
    b. Groundspeed, Ram rise, and true heading
    c. Groundspeed, wind velocity, true heading, and other information
    d. Angle of attack, airspeed, true heading, and other information

16. True airspeed is the same as indicated airspeed in what conditions?
    a. Standard day
    b. Ambient
    c. Completely still
    d. Slower than Mach 1

17. Gyroscopes used in instruments incorporate which two important design characteristics?
    a. Low-density weight for the size and slow rotation
    b. Fixed gimbals and always remaining horizontal
    c. High-density weight for the size and high-speed rotation with no friction
    d. High-density weight for the small size and high-speed rotation with low friction

18. Which of these instruments does not show the relative position of the aircraft with respect to the earth's horizon?
    a. Attitude indicator
    b. Vertical speed indicator
    c. Gyro horizon
    d. Vertical gyro indicator

19. Which of these was one of the first modern instruments for controlling an aircraft without visual reference to the ground or horizon?
    a. Groundspeed indicator
    b. Ring laser gyroscope
    c. Turn and bank indicator
    d. Pitot-static pressure gauge

20. Which of these types of gyroscopes is lighter and simpler than the others because of no need for plumbing and air filters?
    a. Engine-driven vacuum system
    b. Electrically driven system
    c. Venturi-tube system
    d. Vacuum system

21. Which type of solid-state gyroscope uses the Sagnac effect and compares internal light frequencies to detect motion?
    a. MEMS
    b. Strap-down electrical gyroscope
    c. Inertial reference system
    d. Ring laser gyroscope

22. Which gyroscope is integrated into a complete, small, electronic solid-state chip that looks like a tiny circuit board and operates by processing microvoltage signals?
    a. MEMS
    b. Strap-down electrical gyroscope
    c. Inertial reference system
    d. Ring laser gyroscope

Chapter 1
Aircraft Instruments

MULTIPLE CHOICE QUESTIONS

name:

date:

23. What indicator consists of a miniature aircraft symbol, a bank angle dial, a bank index, and a two-colored drum background?
    a. Standby altimeter
    b. Directional gyroscope
    c. Standby attitude indicator
    d. Turn and bank indicator

24. An analog accelerometer uses what type of system to indicate forces on the aircraft?
    a. Gyroscope and gimbal
    b. Fluid and ball
    c. Mass and pulley
    d. Weight and spring

25. Which of these is not a type of clock used in aircraft?
    a. Solar powered analog
    b. Mechanically wound analog
    c. Electrically powered analog
    d. Electrically powered digital

26. One of the flight crew's responsibilities—keeping the engines within operation limits—is now handled by what systems on modern aircraft with electronic controls?
    a. Electrical instrument and engine controls
    b. Full authority digital engine control
    c. Remote engine controls
    d. Automatic engine information feedback

27. Reciprocating engine tachometer indicators have an internal motor that turns at the same rate as what?
    a. The generator mounted to the engine
    b. The propeller
    c. The propeller drive gear
    d. The engine crankshaft

28. A tachometer probe is reliable because, unlike tachometer generators, it has what?
    a. Sealed bearings
    b. Only two gears
    c. A strobe light
    d. No moving parts

29. The rate of fuel flow is displayed in what per hour for turbine engines and in what per hour for reciprocating engines?
    a. Pounds, ounces
    b. Gallons, gallons
    c. Pounds, gallons
    d. Kilograms, liters

30. A thermal dispersion fuel flow transmitter heats fuel at one point and uses what to detect how much the fuel has cooled from that point to further downstream?
    a. Digital thermometers
    b. Mass fuel flowmeters
    c. Hall effect transducers
    d. Resistance temperature detectors

31. Engine oil that is too hot or that is not the right pressure can indicate trouble. Which of these is not a cause for a drop in oil pressure and, thus, impending engine failure?
    a. A lack of oil
    b. Oil that is too hot
    c. Oil pump failure
    d. Broken lines

32. Which turbine engine operating limit is used to monitor the integrity of the turbine, check engine operating conditions, and is the first indication in a startup that the engine has started to run?
    a. N_1 speed
    b. Exhaust gas temperature
    c. N_2 speed
    d. Oil pressure

33. If only one thermocouple is used as a cylinder head temperature sensor, on which cylinder head should it be placed?
    a. Any cylinder
    b. The cylinder that was tested to run the coolest
    c. The cylinder that was tested to run hottest
    d. The cylinder that is furthest aft

34. What characteristics are measured in the two types of torquemeters used in aircraft with turboprop engines?
    a. Shaft speed and oil pressure
    b. Oil pressure and strobe delay
    c. Torsional deflection and oil pressure
    d. Generator amps and strobe delay

Chapter 1
Aircraft Instruments

MULTIPLE CHOICE QUESTIONS

name:

date:

35. Which of these allows the flight crew to monitor a turbine engine's rotating assemblies balance?
    a. N₂ balance gauge
    b. Torsional deflection meter
    c. Synchroscope
    d. Turbine vibration indicator

36. With an ECAM system, what components process information received from the system data analog converter and then forward the information to the signal generators for display on the monitors?
    a. Warning computers
    b. Symbol monitors
    c. Flight phase monitors
    d. Built-in test equipment

37. Which part of an EICAS allows the pilot to choose which computer is the primary for supplying information and what secondary engine information and system status is displayed on the lower monitor.
    a. Display select panel
    b. Manual display mode
    c. Bottom monitor controls
    d. Maintenance panel

38. An EICAS allows the flight crew to record what, such as in a failure event, so that maintenance personnel can check them out later?
    a. Cockpit sounds
    b. Pilot commands issued
    c. Control surface positions
    d. Parameters of the flight

39. One type of fuel quantity system uses a float in the tank, which moves a connecting arm to the wiper on a variable resistor. This resistor is wired in series with one of the coils of what in the instrument panel?
    a. Bourdon tube gauge
    b. Ratiometer fuel gauge
    c. Analog data converter
    d. Piezoelectric meter

40. Several of what basic electrical component are used in the aircraft's landing gear wheel wells for operating the position indicator?
    a. Solenoids
    b. Pressure gauges
    c. Limit switches
    d. Photoelectric sensors

41. What is the range in which an aircraft can receive radio waves from a VOR station?
    a. It depends on the aircraft's direction
    b. 150 miles
    c. 300 miles
    d. 200 miles

42. A VOR receiver can determine the aircraft's deviation off of a VOR station's transmission because the transmitter produces two signals: one as a reference signal, and the second as what?
    a. Variable signal
    b. Pulsed signal
    c. Omni-bearing signal
    d. Latitude/longitude signal

43. VOR receivers are sometime in the same avionics unit as the VHF communication transceivers, which are called what?
    a. NAV/COMM radios
    b. VOR/VHF units
    c. GPS units
    d. VHF/heading radios

44. In the instrument landing system, the localizer antenna broadcasts at a range of between what two frequencies on the odd tenths of the megahertz steps?
    a. 100.0 MHz to 115.0 MHz
    b. 108.0 MHz to 112.0 MHz
    c. 90.0 MHz to 150.0 MHz
    d. 110.0 MHz to 114.0 MHz

45. In the instrument landing system, the glideslope antenna broadcasts at a range of between what two frequencies?
    a. 320.1 MHz to 323.0 MHz
    b. 333.3 MHz to 335.1 MHz
    c. 90 MHz to 150 MHz
    d. 329.3 MHz to 335.0 MHz

Chapter 1
Aircraft Instruments

MULTIPLE CHOICE QUESTIONS

name:

date:

46. The three marker beacons' purpose is to what?
    a. Mark three possible glide paths to the runway
    b. Confirm that the aircraft is at the proper horizontal position and heading at three stages, relative to the runway
    c. Indicate to the flight crew that the aircraft is at the outer, middle, and inner (or threshold) marker locations relative to the runway
    d. Broadcast a signal only if they can verify that the aircraft is at the proper altitude at the outer, middle, and inner locations, relative to the runway.

47. With an automatic direction finder, a loop antenna on the aircraft monitors the strength of the ground station's signal because a radio wave hitting a loop antenna broadside induces a what?
    a. Stronger signal
    b. Null signal
    c. Morse code-like signal of dashes
    d. Magnetic signal

48. Which ground station system returns a signal in response to an aircraft's signal that is modulated with a string of interrogation pulses and then used to calculate nautical miles from the station?
    a. Instrument landing system
    b. Glideslope and sense loop system
    c. Radio magnetic pulse equipment
    d. Distance measuring equipment

49. Global positioning system has several limitations. Which one of the following should global positioning systems not be used to perform?
    a. Avoid other aircraft in navigation
    b. Measure distance to the runway
    c. Fly an approach and land
    d. Navigate a route

50. Which of these is not an advantage of electronic flight instrument systems over traditional analog instruments?
    a. No calibration is needed
    b. Less complex, and simpler mounting and wiring
    c. Lower maintenance costs and better dispatch reliability
    d. Larger, easier-to-read displays

51. Early electronic flight instrument systems displayed this combination, known as an electronic attitude director indicator, which includes what indications?
    a. Turn and bank, compass, airspeed, and altitude
    b. Gyro horizon, directional gyros, airspeed, and altitude
    c. Gyro horizon, vertical speed, compass, and altitude
    d. Compass, latitude/longitude, airspeed, and angle of attack

52. The flight director performs what function for the flight crew?
    a. Signals how to steer for a flight maneuver
    b. Provides text commands for the next heading
    c. Shows an airplane symbol on a moving map with the flight path to follow
    d. Shows taxiways and runways to take while on the ground

53. An electronic horizontal situation indicator can operate in what modes?
    a. Navigation, VOR, weather, and ILS
    b. Map, VOR, and ILS
    c. Plan, map, VOR, and ILS
    d. Weather, navigation, DME, and ILS

54. Who is permitted to repair faulty instruments?
    a. Only airframe and powerplant (A&P) certified personnel
    b. Anyone, as long as the FAA approves the instrument before it is put into service
    c. Only Aviation Maintenance Technicians (AMT) or Avionics Electronics Technicians (AET)
    d. Only repair facilities that are certified FAA repair stations

55. Which of these is not a feature that instrument panels incorporate to make the instruments more readable?
    a. Dull black paint
    b. Double panels
    c. Glareshield
    d. Anti-glare coating

Chapter 1
Aircraft Instruments

MULTIPLE CHOICE QUESTIONS

name:

date:

56. What is a great resource for determining how to fix an analog gauge, for example?
    a. Built-in test equipment
    b. Aircraft maintenance panel display
    c. Troubleshooting chart or table
    d. Ohmmeters and pressure gauges

57. In which procedure might you see a person standing in front of an aircraft, and another person in the cockpit coordinating with each other with hand signals to adjust an aircraft's position?
    a. Compass swing
    b. Compass rose calibration
    c. Pitot-static test
    d. General, preflight check

Chapter 1
Aircraft Instruments

ANALYSIS QUESTIONS

name:

date:

1. Most modern instruments use two components. What are these components, and what is the function of each?

2. A proximity switch/sensor can be used in systems where it is desirable to detect the position of a part without making actual physical contact. On what aircraft systems would this technology provide an advantage? Why?

3. Numeric displays are very popular because they provide precise measurements in an easy-to-read form. What technology can be used to drive this type of display?

4. On many modern aircraft the individual wires connecting sensors and displays have been replaced with a single data bus. Briefly explain the operation of a data bus.

Chapter 1
Aircraft Instruments

ANALYSIS QUESTIONS

name:

date:

5. The pitot-static system provides ram air and static air for use in certain instruments. What are the three primary instruments connected to this system, and to which air source is each connected?

6. Machmeters are designed to compare the speed of the aircraft with the speed of sound. Because the speed of sound becomes slower as altitude increases, the instrument must compensate for this to give an accurate reading. What design feature of the machmeter compensates for the change in value due to altitude?

7. Aircraft flying at 0.8 Mach and higher can experience pressure building up on the aircraft's skin. These pressures distort the normal airflow and cause false pressure readings from the pitot-static system. What system is generally installed on these aircraft to compensate for this, and what types of inputs are used to ensure accurate outputs?

8. A standard aneroid type altimeter uses air pressure to display the aircraft's altitude above mean sea level. The radar (or radio) altimeter does not rely on the pitot-static pressure system for determining altitude. What altitude information is provided by this system, and how is altitude determined?

9. Gyroscopes have traditionally been used in several aircraft instruments. What are the two basic properties of gyroscopic action and how are they used to make gyroscopes useful aircraft instruments?

10. Microelectromechanical sensors (MEMS) are the latest in solid-state gyro technology. Briefly explain the construction and the operating principles of these chips.

11. Tachometers are used to measure engine speed, in both reciprocating and turbine engines. Explain what is actually being monitored in each type of engine, and what units are seen on the tachometer dial for each type of engine.

12. Thermocouples are used to measure the temperature of exhaust gases in both turbine and reciprocating engines and other applications where temperature measurement is needed. Briefly explain the operating principle of a thermocouple temperature indicating system.

Chapter 1
Aircraft Instruments

ANALYSIS QUESTIONS

name:

date:

Chapter 1
Aircraft Instruments

ANALYSIS QUESTIONS

name:

date:

13. The VHF Omnidirectional Range navigation system is commonly used on both large and small aircraft. This system gives the pilot information regarding the aircraft's position relative to the station, and whether its movement is TO or FROM that station. Briefly explain the operating principle of the VOR.

14. The Instrument Landing System (ILS) is used to guide aircraft to a safe landing. It is referred to as a "system" because it uses several separate components. Identify each of the components used in an ILS and briefly explain the function of each.

15. Global positioning system (GPS) use is increasing. Explain briefly how a simple GPS can provide both aircraft location and height above the ground.

16. Colored range markings and limits help the pilot quickly differentiate between normal and abnormal situations. The most common markings are a green arc, a yellow arc, a white arc, and a red radial line. Briefly explain what each one of these markings indicate.

Chapter 2
Radar Systems

FILL IN THE BLANK QUESTIONS

name:

date:

1. Flight crews are trained to use weather radar to avoid convective weather by steering to the _____ side of the storm and avoiding the area by a minimum of _____ NM.

2. _____ is the one type of precipitation that has the least reflectivity to the weather radar transmitted pulse.

3. The time it takes radio frequency energy to travel 1 NM, reflect off an object, and the echo signal to travel back 1 NM mile is _____.

4. Transmitter power of an airborne weather radar system is measured in _____ power.

5. Pulse width (PW) refers to the _____ of the pulse of energy emitted from the radar antenna, and PRT refers to _____.

6. In a radar system, the unit tasked with generating the transmitted pulse and then preparing the resulting echo signal for the display is referred to as the _____.

7. The internal _____ signal's primary purpose is to provide a means of synchronizing the elements in that radar system for transmitting and collecting radar target data.

8. The _____ consists of a cathode, interaction space, and an anode that houses resonant cavities around its internal circumference.

9. A/An _____ functions as a transmission line that has been adapted for use with the high frequencies of the microwave frequency spectrum.

10. Antenna stabilization, controlled by sensing the real-time pitch and roll attitude of the aircraft, adds an additional _____ of antenna tilt to the pilot-controlled ±15° of manual antenna tilt.

11. _____ is a technique to equalize the echo signals for the first 25 NM to 50 NM of range so that storms that are closer to the aircraft do not appear larger than they actually are.

12. An analog radar system receives the echo signal and passes it directly to the weather radar _____ for display.

13. The electron stream created in a cathode ray tube (CRT) holds a negative potential and operates under the principles of _____ attracts and _____ repels.

Chapter 2
Radar Systems

FILL IN THE BLANK QUESTIONS

name:

date:

14. In an analog radar system, the ISO-contour mode displays thunderstorms of a certain size, or larger, with a black center or reverse video. The minimum value of _____ _____ is the average onset of vertical, developed, cumulonimbus cloud formations that are considered a threat to the aircraft.

15. In early digital radar systems, the receiver-transmitter's video detector converts the echo signal into video; amplifies it, integrates it, and then detects its level; and then converts it into digital binary _____ outputs.

16. The display technique used to collect and display digitized weather data is called the _____ .

17. When a color radar display is operated in a weather mode, _____ represents the storm category of Extreme-Intense or more than _____ per hour of rainfall.

18. Even though it is somewhat rudimentary, a radar's _____ allows the flight crew to effectively differentiate among rivers, lakes, shorelines, and urban centers.

19. The flight crew can adjust the displayed distance of weather radar targets, typically in preset distances from 5 NM to 300 NM using the _____ .

20. To display the intended navigation plot along with weather targets correlated in real-time, modern radar systems incorporate external navigation data from a/an _____ _____ .

21. Some weather radar systems have a/an _____ mode that relies on the Doppler shift effect caused by the motion or velocity of detected weather.

22. Testing a weather radar system incorrectly, such as using the Test function while the aircraft is in the hangar, can be harmful and result in _____ .

23. A good way to determine test procedures that are unique and applicable to the aircraft is to use the radar system manufacturer's _____ .

24. Flight crews might typically report any number of radar failures with one phrase, commenting that the radar is _____ .

25. An automatic frequency control out-of-lock condition appears as _____ _____ appearing for an instant or flashing randomly on the radar display.

26. _____ can manifest as random curved spokes with a dashed line-like appearance called rabbit tracking.

Chapter 2
Radar Systems

MULTIPLE CHOICE QUESTIONS

name:

date:

1. A radar system fundamentally consists of which three main components?
   a. Transponder, antenna, and indicator (display)
   b. Receiver-transmitter, antenna with a waveguide, and indicator (display)
   c. Waveguide, antenna, and indicator (display)
   d. Transponder, analog-to-digital converter, and indicator (display)

2. The transmitter produces a high-power pulse of radio frequency at what frequency and for approximately what duration or pulse width?
   a. 9.375 GHz; 3 to 4 microseconds
   b. 19.5 GHz; 3 to 4 microseconds
   c. 9.375 MHz; 3 to 4 seconds
   d. 9.375 GHz; 10 to 12 milliseconds

3. The formula, $R = c \Delta t / 2$, is used to calculate what?
   a. The speed of light
   b. The speed a storm or object is traveling
   c. The range or distance to a storm or object
   d. The time it will take to reach a storm or object

4. What are the most common sizes for a radar antenna on large, transport aircraft?
   a. Between 18 and 24 inches
   b. Between 16 and 32 inches
   c. Between 20 and 22 inches
   d. Between 18 and 22 inches

5. What two factors most affect a radar system's operational range?
   a. Pulse width and antenna size
   b. Antenna shape and receiver's ability to receive weak signals
   c. Antenna size and computer's ability to filter out atmospheric noise
   d. Transmitter peak power and receiver's sensitivity (ability to receive weak signals)

6. What occurrence is described as a distant target that could appear as a weak, short-range target in a subsequent pulse transmission?
   a. Short echo trace
   b. False trace
   c. Receiver-induced echo
   d. Second trace echo

7. In a magnetron, where the 9.375 MHz of electromagnetic energy is created, the resonant cavities form part of which internal component?
   a. Interaction space
   b. Cathode
   c. Permanent magnet
   d. Anode

8. A radio frequency pulse generated by the magnetron is directed through this component and then passed on to the antenna for transmission?
   a. Coaxial cable
   b. 12-gauge wire
   c. Pulse-to-digital converter
   d. Waveguide

9. Which type of antenna design is considered obsolete, and what is the name of the newer, more efficient design?
   a. Parabolic dish reflector, and the planar array or flat plate
   b. Parabolic dish, and waveguide
   c. Waveguide, and planar array
   d. Feed horn, and waveguide

10. The magnetron has a tendency to drift off center frequency. What is required to counteract this and to calibrate the returning echo signals for attenuation caused by atmospheric signal loss?
    a. Antenna stabilization and sensitivity time control
    b. Automatic frequency control and sensitivity time control
    c. Automatic gain control and duplexer
    d. Duplexer and second trace echo

11. What is the result when the radar system's mixer combines the local oscillator's output with the echo signal?
    a. Frequency steering pulses
    b. A steady varactor diode current
    c. An intermediate frequency of 60 MHz
    d. Gunn diode limiting pulses

Chapter 2
Radar Systems

MULTIPLE CHOICE QUESTIONS

name:

date:

12. Which of the following best describes the automatic frequency control unit's function?
    a. Controls the pulse width and pulse repetition frequency so they are not too wide or frequent
    b. Limits the antenna's range to 120° of sweep
    c. Ensures that the range of frequency generated by the magnetron is within 30 GHz of 9.345 GHz.
    d. Manages the magnetron's frequency variance by sampling a small portion of each transmitted pulse and recalibrating the receiver local oscillator injection frequency

13. Two types of automatic frequency control circuits are used: one with a transmit-receive (TR) limiting microwave device (or TR limiter) at the input of the receiver, and the second is one with?
    a. Capacitive elements and baffles (matching iris) as inductive elements sealed in a gas-filled cavity
    b. Microprocessor technology to detect the peak level of receiver output
    c. An antenna sweep-limiting mechanism to narrow the pulse's focus
    d. An analog-to-digital converter at the receiver input

14. The automatic gain control unit measures receiver noise just before the RF pulse is transmitted, to determine the receiver noise band level and set the what?
    a. Receiver output level
    b. Atmospheric reserve threshold
    c. Receiver gain threshold
    d. Receiver-transmitter decibel levels

15. Which radar system RT component allows the antenna to be used to both transmit the RF pulse and receive the echo signal?
    a. Duplexer
    b. TR limiter
    c. Local oscillator
    d. Automatic gain control

16. What type of display is used in an analog radar system?
    a. Multifunction display
    b. Light emitting diode display
    c. Liquid crystal display
    d. Cathode ray tube

17. In a cathode ray tube, the electron gun shoots an electron beam toward a phosphor-coated glass screen. What directs this stream of electrons to their correct location on the screen?
    a. Horizontal deflection plates only
    b. Horizontal and vertical deflection plates
    c. Vertical deflection plates only
    d. An anode loop

18. Which one of the following radar receiver-transmitter circuits is responsible for digitizing the detected video output of the receiver?
    a. Sensitivity time control (STC)
    b. Analog-to-digital converter
    c. Automatic frequency control (AFC)
    d. Automatic gain control (AGC)

19. What term is used to describe the process when Rho-Theta accumulated radar data is scan converted so that each memory location is assigned to a display cell represented by a row and column?
    a. Electron beam scan
    b. X-Y raster scan
    c. X-Y vector scan
    d. 3D scan

20. The antenna sensor design has a microprocessor that formats the detected weather video output to a Rho-Theta format and then encodes the data to what digital format signal before sending it to the indicator on an ARINC 453 data bus?
    a. ARINC 708
    b. ARINC 453
    c. X-Y raster
    d. 3-D vector

21. Why does a radar system have a 90- to 120-second standby status when it is first turned on?
    a. To warm up the antenna stabilization mechanism
    b. To allow time for the initial echo signals to be processed
    c. To prevent an X-band microwave radiation hazard on the ground
    d. To give the magnetron time to reach its operating temperature

Chapter 2
Radar Systems

MULTIPLE CHOICE QUESTIONS

name:

date:

22. When a radar system is in weather mode, what is the term to describe the degree of rainfall rate (represented by Z) from a target using a decibel (dB) logarithmic scale in decibels relative to Z (dBZ)?
    a. Movement
    b. Density
    c. Reflectivity
    d. Opacity

23. Which sequence of colors depicts the weather radar storm category thresholds in order of weakest to strongest?
    a. Black, yellow, green, red, flashing red
    b. Black, green, yellow, red, magenta
    c. Black, yellow, green, red, flashing red
    d. Magenta, red, green yellow, black

24. What feature allows the flight crew to adjust the antenna pitch by ±15° to assess the vertical profile of a developing weather target?
    a. Lateral sweep control
    b. Local oscillator control
    c. Tilt control
    d. Antenna stabilization control

25. Which of these is one company's name of a feature that highlights the shadow area behind a storm with a cyan color on the radar indicator to represent the radar's inability to effectively paint targets in that range?
    a. Rain attenuation shadow compensation technique (RASCT)
    b. Rain echo attenuation compensation technique (REACT)
    c. Rain shadow calculation
    d. Rain echo blocking attenuation technique (REBAT)

26. What advanced feature automatically helps a flight crew understand a target's vertical profile and development and, thus, its threat level?
    a. Vertical profile mode
    b. Automatic tilt control mode
    c. Tilt automation mode (TAM)
    d. Vertical automatic profile

27. FAA Advisory Circular AC 20-68B highlights the danger that exists when operating an aircraft's radar system while on the ground and defines the what?
    a. Allowed exposure level (AEL)
    b. Maximum permissible exposure level (MPEL)
    c. Proximity allowable level (PAL)
    d. Safe allowable exposure level (SEAL)

28. What are the dangers of testing a radar system inside a hangar?
    a. It could damage equipment and human eyes
    b. It can cause liquids to boil and damage human reproductive organs
    c. It can ignite combustible material and give nearby humans heartburn
    d. It could ignite combustible material and damage nearby persons' eyes and reproductive organs

29. What kind of test involves positioning the radar to its maximum up tilt position, and repeatedly lowering the tilt control until below +5° and reducing the range to eventually display ground returns?
    a. Radar test mode
    b. Safe ground test mode
    c. Radar ground functional test
    d. Radar weather mode test

30. Spoking can be caused by what?
    a. Natural attenuation and radome damage
    b. Snow and cold weather systems
    c. Magnetron failure only
    d. Numerous random external effects or internal defects

31. Two common internal defects that can cause spoking are what?
    a. Weak magnetron pulse, and transmitter pulse width is shorter than 3.5 μsec
    b. AFC is out of lock, and antenna stabilization control problems
    c. Receiver sensitivity is outside a range of between -100 and -110 dBm, and sensitivity time control is out of adjustment
    d. Antenna stabilization control problems, and transmitter pulse width is shorter than 3.5 μsec

Chapter 2
Radar Systems

MULTIPLE CHOICE QUESTIONS

name:

date:

32. What can cause a symptom called frequency pulling, which briefly causes the RT to be de-tuned, creating a situation that is beyond the limits of the AFC circuit?
    a. Moisture inside the radome because of poor maintenance
    b. AFC being out of lock
    c. Receiver sensitivity is outside a range of between -100 and -110 dBm,
    d. Sensitivity time control being out of adjustment

Chapter 2
Radar Systems

ANALYSIS QUESTIONS

name:

date:

1. What effect does increasing a radar system's antenna dish diameter have on the transmitted RF energy and what performance benefit or benefits are realized by a larger diameter antenna?

2. When a manufacturer designs a weather radar system capable of varying the pulse width of the transmitted RF energy, at what range does a narrower pulse width give the greatest performance gain?

3. What two radar parameters combine to defeat second trace echo?

4. What immediate troubleshooting action should a technician take if a flight crew reports that artifacts are painted on the weather radar indicator in front of the aircraft where no observable item or weather system is visible or reported?

5. What influence would the loss of the vertical gyro input have on a weather radar system?

6. One notable characteristic of the magnetron in a weather radar system is a magnetron's tendency to wander in frequency over time. What weather radar circuit compensates for this minor variation in output frequency?

Chapter 2
Radar Systems

ANALYSIS QUESTIONS

name:

date:

7. Radio receiver sensitivity is determined using a signal-to-noise ratio ($S + N / N$) measurement; however, weather radar sensitivity is expressed and measured using minimum detectable signal (MDS). Why is a signal-to-noise ratio an unworkable measurement technique in a weather radar system?

8. What is the purpose of measuring the Doppler frequency shift of the reflected echo signal?

9. Why is operating a weather radar system in Test mode not a recommended practice when an aircraft is in the hangar?

10. A flight crew reports that the weather radar does not appear to be painting weather targets and intermittently flashes radial lines at different azimuths. What possible condition exists, and what action should the technician take to fix this fault?

Chapter 3
Air Traffic Surveillance and Warning

FILL IN THE BLANK QUESTIONS

name:

date:

1. The main reason having air traffic control and for developing surveillance and warning systems is to _____ .

2. A radar system that is on the ground and can determine aircraft location (even azimuth) is called a/an _____ system.

3. The airborne portion of a secondary surveillance radar (SSR) system receives coded air traffic control requests and transmits a reply of a code using the aircraft's _____ .

4. As part of Mode S SSR equipment on the aircraft, a radio beacon called a/an _____ can transmit and receive many types of aircraft tracking data.

5. Name at least three of the types of information a Mode S transponder can transmit:
   _____
   _____

6. The ground SSR system determines the mode, or the interrogation, by the amount of time between the pulses, which are called _____ and _____ .

7. Another pulse from the SSR system, known as _____, is broadcast in an omnidirectional pattern 2 µS after the first pulse and is used to ensure that the transponder replies only to the _____ .

8. The data from false types of SSR transmissions show as flickering and intermittent targets on the PPI and are called _____
   _____ .

9. Transmissions to Mode S transponders are called _____, and transmissions from a Mode S transponder are called _____ .

10. In a Mode S transmission from the ground, the P6 pulse is _____ long and is phase shift keyed; it can contain _____, called chips.

11. Transmissions from transponders are sent on a radio frequency of _____ .

12. In a Mode-C transmission, the aircraft's pressure altitude and other information is sent after it is encoded into the _____ .

13. In a Mode S transponder downlink, the information in the data block is encoded using the _____ .

14. Aircraft with Mode S transponders have a/an _____, which allows ATC to uplink to and download from an aircraft individually.

Chapter 3
Air Traffic Surveillance and Warning

FILL IN THE BLANK QUESTIONS

name:

date:

15. ATC instructions are sent in Mode S uplinks in a/an _____ and are divided into several uplink messages.

16. Small aircraft equipped with distance measuring equipment might be equipped with a/an _____ , which allows only the DME or SSR transponder to transmit at a time. This prevents interference problems.

17. If ATC asks the flight crew to identify (IDENT), the crew then presses the transponder's identification switch. This causes the transponder to turn on the _____ _____ pulse for about 20 seconds, which shows the aircraft's identity on the ATC display.

18. Super-heterodyne receivers tune in different frequencies and convert them to a/an _____ for further processing.

19. The _____ inside a transponder uses control head squawk code or altitude information and creates a reply or downlink, which is sent by the _____ to the antenna.

20. For transponders, the FAA made _____ that are more rigorous than other avionics.

21. The FAA categorizes transponders at several _____ and within those into _____ .

22. The _____ can exchange extended length messages and Comm-B communications with multiple Mode S interrogators at a time.

23. When testing a transponder's All Call decoding, the transponder should withhold a downlink when it receives a/an _____ message and downlink when it receives a/an _____ message.

24. If an aircraft is capable of receiving a recommendation that is issued to change altitude, known as a/an _____ , to avoid a midair collision with another aircraft, you know that the equipment is using traffic collision and avoidance system (TCAS) II.

25. TCAS II antennas consist of a directional antenna that is mounted on the top of the aircraft, and _____ mounted on the bottom.

26. Overlapping replies or downlinks, which are called _____ , are reduced by using directional antennas and partitioning the messages.

27. The TCAS traffic display uses _____ to indicate the threat status of other nearby aircraft.

28. A TCAS also provides _____ when a TA or RA is issued because of nearby traffic.

29. An approximation of the time (in seconds) to the closest point of approach or to the aircraft being at the same altitude is called _____ .

30. To resolve an encounter with another TCAS II-equipped intruder, a TCAS II sends _____ containing information about an aircraft's intended RA sense.

31. ADS depends on the aircraft's _____ , which is why the system is referred to as automatic dependent surveillance.

32. In the 1090ES ADS-B Out type of system, it broadcasts using the transmitter at 1,090 MHz, and the ES stands for _____ .

33. In the second ADS-B Out form of system, it broadcasts with a device called a universal access transceiver (UAT) that operates at _____ MHz.

34. The typical ADS-B system is connected to an appropriate _____ _____ to report its horizontal position.

35. To avoid transmitting conflicting data, a 978 UAT ADS-B transmitter may use a system, called _____ , to detect the transponder downlinks or replies.

36. In aircraft on transoceanic routes, the ADS communicates with ATC via a/an _____ .

37. A/An _____ system takes position information received on the ground from UAT-equipped aircraft and rebroadcasts it.

38. Aircraft using a 1090ES system for both ADS-B Out and In can receive _____ only on the ADS-B In and cannot receive _____ .

Chapter 3
Air Traffic Surveillance and Warning

FILL IN THE BLANK QUESTIONS

name:

date:

Chapter 3
Air Traffic Surveillance and Warning

MULTIPLE CHOICE QUESTIONS

name:

date:

1. In a primary surveillance radar (PSR) system, the directional antenna is connected to a display screen that shows aircraft locations. This display is the PPI, which stands for what?
   a. Plan position indicator
   b. Planar position inclination
   c. Position plane indicator
   d. Planned position inspector

2. The original radar system, known as primary surveillance radar (PSR), is called what in the military?
   a. Identity system one (ISO)
   b. Identification and azimuth (IAA)
   c. Airborne identity system (AIS)
   d. Identification-friend or foe (IFF)

3. Which SSR mode allows the aircraft to reply with crosslink (collision avoidance) information?
   a. Crosslink A
   b. Shortform mode A
   c. Mode S long format
   d. ATCR1 mode

4. In a ground SSR transmitter, the radiation pattern's main transmission is straight, but the transmitter also has energy leakage called what?
   a. Side lobes
   b. P2 energy
   c. Ancillary lobes
   d. Parallel energy

5. After the FAA has obtained the data necessary for flight tracking, what is the name of the standard that prevents a transponder from transmitting, as a way to reduce the number of transmissions?
   a. Chatter suppression logic
   b. Lockout protocol
   c. Duplicates monitoring software
   d. Redundancy reduction algorithm

6. To perform side lobe suppression, which pulse in ATCRBS transponders and which pulse in Mode S transponders are calibrated such that any response to a ground interrogation anywhere except in the main lobe is suppressed?
   a. SLS2, and SLS5
   b. PP, and SLS
   c. P2, and P5
   d. P3, and P6

7. In an ATCRBS transponder, all numeric pulses for the four-digit reply in modes 1 through B are bounded by which two pulses, which are also known as what?
   a. B1 and B2, bounding pulses
   b. F1 and F2, framing pulses
   c. 1 and B, boundary pulses
   d. F1 and F5, border pulses

8. In a Mode S transponder, information is broadcast in a once-per-second downlink beacon, called a what?
   a. Splitter
   b. Squawker
   c. Beacon
   d. Squitter

9. With a Mode S transponder, the information that is traded between aircraft and ground stations is referred to as a what?
   a. Datalink
   b. Data exchange
   c. Metadata
   d. Transmittal

10. When the SSR uses a Mode S uplink for enhanced surveillance, the process is referred to as a/an what?
    a. SSR system exchange (SSE)
    b. Ground initiated comm B (GICB)
    c. Land-based surveillance response (LBSR)
    d. Extended squitter exchange (ESE)

11. When a Mode S transponder is in GND mode, the vertical status bit is set to show that the aircraft is on the ground. Some units switch to this mode automatically from input by what?
    a. Altimeter
    b. Flight information system
    c. Attitude heading reference system (AHRS)
    d. Weight on wheels (WOW) sensor

Chapter 3
Air Traffic Surveillance and Warning

MULTIPLE CHOICE QUESTIONS

name:

date:

12. The local oscillator (LO) in a super-heterodyne receiver provides the mixer with a frequency to combine with the incoming RF. The heterodyning action produces which four unique frequencies at the mixer output to send to the receiver's intermediate frequency (IF) unit?
    a. IF, Mixer RF, LO, and Sum (IF + LO) frequency
    b. RF, IF, Filtered RF, and Filtered LO
    c. RF, LO frequency, Sum (RF + LO) frequency, and Difference (RF – LO) frequency
    d. Mixer RF modulated, LO, IF, and Sum (IF + LO + RF) frequency

13. When compared to other super-heterodyne receivers, transponder receivers have an additional circuit, known as what, that monitors the output and controls the gain of the IF?
    a. Automatic gain control (AGC)
    b. Automatic overload control (AOC)
    c. Automatic gain and overload control (AGOC)
    d. Heterodyne controller

14. What is one example of why the FAA requires that a transponder meet tolerances for frequency, sensitivity, power output, decoding, and encoding?
    a. A transmitter frequency out of tolerance could report the wrong altitude.
    b. A transmitter frequency out of tolerance could cause the aircraft to appear on the ATC display in multiple locations.
    c. A transmitter frequency out of tolerance could cause the aircraft to crash.
    d. A transmitter frequency out of tolerance could cause the aircraft to be invisible to SSR, without either the pilot or the ATC staff knowing why.

15. The regulations at FAR 91.411 ensure that aircraft operate in controlled airspace under instrument flight rules only if what items have been tested and found to comply with FAR Part 43, appendix E, which specifies tolerances for leaks and accuracy?
    a. Pitot-static system, GPS, and TCAS
    b. GPS, TCAS, and ADS-B Out
    c. Altimeter, static system, and altitude reporting system
    d. Altimeter, GPS, and altitude reporting system

16. Level 1 transponder supports the surveillance functions of both ATCRBS and Mode S, when the uplink or interrogation comes from what source?
    a. Ground and airborne
    b. Ground
    c. Airborne
    d. SATCOM

17. What is the lowest level of transponder that can receive ELM from ground sources?
    a. Level 3
    b. Level 2
    c. Level 4
    d. Level 1

18. Appendix F of FAR Part 43 requires certain transponder tests. Which of the following are not listed in appendix F?
    a. Illumination test
    b. Current draw
    c. Power-on delay
    d. All the above

19. When testing an ATC transponder while it is still in the aircraft, to properly measure MTL and power output, you must enter what into the test set?
    a. Data about the antenna make, model and serial number; aircraft altitude at present; and the distance between the test set antenna and the antenna on the aircraft.
    b. Only the transponder's serial number
    c. Data about the antenna gain, antenna cable loss, aircraft antenna height, and the distance between the test set antenna and the antenna on the aircraft
    d. The altitude of the aircraft where it is sitting

20. Proximity warnings of nearby traffic that help a pilot visually acquire nearby aircraft are called what and are provided by TCAS I?
    a. Visual flight rules (VFR)
    b. Traffic advisories (TA)
    c. SATCOM warnings
    d. 1090 ES warnings

Chapter 3
Air Traffic Surveillance and Warning

MULTIPLE CHOICE QUESTIONS

name:

date:

21. Which component of a TCAS performs surveillance, tracks intruder aircraft, tracks its own altitude, detects threats, determines RA maneuvers, and generates RAs?
    a. TA/RA sensor
    b. Processor or computer
    c. Mode S transponder
    d. Control panel

22. A Mode S transponder is required to provide air-to-air data exchange between TCAS II-equipped aircraft so that coordinated, complementary RAs can be issued when required, which can be referred to as what?
    a. Flight coordination
    b. Area charting
    c. Crosslink
    d. Complementary flying

23. What TCAS component allows the flight crew to place the system in different modes, therefore controlling its operation?
    a. Standby knob
    b. TCAS processor
    c. TCAS voice command processor
    d. Control panel

24. Aircraft TCAS antennas transmit interrogations at what MHz and receive transponder replies or downlinks at what MHz?
    a. 1,090 and 1,030
    b. 978 and 1,030
    c. 1,030 and 1,090
    d. 987 and 1,090

25. What are two displays called that the TCAS uses to inform the pilots of traffic status?
    a. Traffic display and ATC display
    b. Traffic display and resolution advisory display
    c. ATC display and SATCOM display
    d. Resolution advisory display and prime display

26. How is the RTCA document DO-185 relevant to airborne TCAS?
    a. It sets the standards for symbols and colors used on the TCAS displays
    b. It sets the standards for the voice callout wording
    c. It is not relevant; DO-185 is about avoiding weather
    d. It instructs flight crews on how to read displays

27. Airborne TCAS target surveillance provides a range of reliable support up to how far and can track how many transponder-equipped aircraft?
    a. 10 NM, 0.3 aircraft per square nautical mile
    b. 14 NM, 0.3 aircraft per square nautical mile
    c. 12 NM, 1.5 aircraft per square nautical mile
    d. 15 NM, 2.5 aircraft per square nautical mile

28. To determine all alerting functions, TCAS II uses what concept?
    a. TA
    b. Rate × time = distance
    c. 1090ES
    d. Tau

29. If two TCAS II-equipped aircraft simultaneously declare each other as threats and determine identical RAs, what happens next?
    a. The aircraft with the highest Mode S address reverses its sense.
    b. The aircraft with the lowest Mode S address reverses its sense.
    c. The aircraft at the highest altitude reverses its sense.
    d. The aircraft with the lowest heading number reverses its sense.

30. When testing a TCAS, what other aircraft systems must be working?
    a. Altimeter and transponder
    b. SATCOM system
    c. Flight management computer, central maintenance computer, air data system, transponder, and autonomous navigation system
    d. Transponder and ADF

Chapter 3
Air Traffic Surveillance and Warning

MULTIPLE CHOICE QUESTIONS

name:

date:

31. Which of the following data is something that ADS-B does not send out when the aircraft is airborne?
    a. Horizontal position in latitude and longitude
    b. Pressure altitude
    c. Vertical status
    d. Heading

32. What horizontal position accuracy value of the Navigation Integrity Category (NIC) is required for a navigation source used with ADS-B?
    a. 3
    b. 9
    c. 10
    d. 7

33. What does the FAA require if the ADS-B system cannot broadcast all the required data?
    a. That the flight crew be informed
    b. That the emergency code be broadcast at a minimum
    c. That the TCAS processor be rebooted
    d. That the altitude be broadcast at a minimum

34. Which of these best describes ADS-B in?
    a. The receiver portion of the transponder
    b. The part of the ADS system used to send information to the flight crew
    c. The control panel that the flight crew uses to input data
    d. The antennas that receive data

35. TIS-B is a traffic advisory service that provides the altitude, ground track, speed, and distance of aircraft flying in radar contact with controllers and for aircraft within what range and elevation of the receiving aircraft?
    a. A 20-NM radius and up to 2,000 ft. above or below
    b. A 30-NM radius and up to 3,000 ft. above or below
    c. A 10-NM radius and up to 1,500 ft. above or below
    d. A 15-NM radius and up to 3,500 ft. above or below

36. The ADS-B In service providing weather, NOTAMS, and PIREPS is called what?
    a. Traffic Information Service–Broadcast (TIS-B)
    b. ADS-B Info
    c. Flight Information Service–Broadcast (FIS-B)
    d. ADS-B Pilot Info

37. What equipment is needed to receive FIS-B service?
    a. A 1090ES transponder
    b. A 978 MHz UAT
    c. A Mode S transponder
    d. All the above

38. In aircraft receiving both FIS-B and TIS-B, what units display the data to the flight crew?
    a. Navigation system or position source display
    b. A wireless connection to an electronic tablet
    c. Multifunction display
    d. All the above

39. If ADS-B In equipment is integrated with TCAS, what is not required for airborne traffic?
    a. ACARS operation
    b. TIS-B reception
    c. FIS-B reception
    d. CDTI operation

Chapter 3
Air Traffic Surveillance and Warning

ANALYSIS QUESTIONS

name:

date:

1. Regardless of the number settings on the control head, a transponder transmits only 2, 3, 5, 6, and 7 as a first digit in Mode A. What is the most likely problem?

2. Air traffic control reports a transponder replies with random and incorrect altitudes at certain times and, at others, does not reply with any altitude. What is the most likely problem?

3. In flight, the transponder reply light remains on constantly, and yet air traffic control reports the aircraft is not visible on SSR. In addition, the DME does not lock onto a nearby station. What is the most likely problem?

4. A transponder does not reply to a Mode C interrogation, but it does report altitude on the faceplate and during the appropriate Mode S downlink. Where is the most likely problem?

5. A transponder does not downlink to a mode S uplink, but it does work normally in modes A and C. Where is the most likely problem?

6. What effect could a dirty and greasy antenna have on a transponder?

Chapter 3
Air Traffic Surveillance and Warning

ANALYSIS QUESTIONS

name:

date:

7. A TCAS II does not give a coordinated RA for an aircraft equipped with a TCAS I. Why would this be the case?

8. A TCAS II does not give an RA for an aircraft equipped with an ATCRBS transponder without an altitude encoding device. Why would this be the case?

9. Two TCAS II-equipped aircraft declare each other as threats simultaneously. The TCAS II in both aircraft determine an RA requiring a climb and broadcast their intent message simultaneously. What is the final tie breaking process to ensure both flight crews do not receive the same RA?

10. A TCAS cannot be switched out of standby mode. When troubleshooting, what is the next course of action?

11. What problem could cause a 978 UAT to transmit a different code than the ATC transponder?

12. If no ADS-B test equipment is available, by what means can someone get a verified test of an ADS-B system?

Chapter 4
Weather and Terrain Awareness and Avoidance

FILL IN THE BLANK QUESTIONS

name:

date:

1. _____ provide specialized briefings and tailored forecasts to support the needs of the FAA and other users of the National Airspace System.

2. Significant Meteorological Information (SIGMETs) and Airmen's Meteorological Information (AIRMETs) are two examples of _____.

3. The FAA's extensive surface weather observing program provides airport observations (METAR and SPECI), which are made by _____.

4. Flight service stations (FSS) can give briefings to flight crews while in flight. Pilots may contact the FSS on the _____ frequency, give their location, and receive the briefing.

5. RRTNM stands for _____. Radar systems use it to compute distance by dividing elapsed time by RRTNM, which is 12.36 microseconds.

6. Most airborne weather radar systems operate at _____ GHz frequency, which is in the _____, a subset of frequencies in the super high-frequency band.

7. In monochrome radar displays, contour cyclic mode cycles the contour mode on and off, which causes the intense precipitation to _____.

8. A type of distortion, called _____, makes objects appear wider than they are and is a result of the radio energy spreading out as it leaves the antenna.

9. As a radar signal passes through precipitation, it _____.

10. The sudden change in wind velocity or direction that is a hazard to low-flying aircraft and when on an approach to a runway is called _____.

11. _____ systems, also known as passive weather detection systems, detect lightning from storms and are popular for use on small aircraft because of their light weight and low cost.

12. The type of system that is the answer to question 11 detects lightning by monitoring for _____ kHz signals and by using a/an _____ antenna to detect the lightning's azimuth.

13. A skin mapper allows you to _____ for electrical noise before mounting the antenna.

14. NEXRAD, which stands for _____, creates a/an _____ by combining the results of several radar scans.

Chapter 4
Weather and Terrain Awareness and Avoidance

FILL IN THE BLANK QUESTIONS

name:

date:

15. NEXRAD transmitters that alternate between horizontally polarized and vertically polarized pulses use what is called _____, which allows the system to differentiate between snow, hail, ice pellets, and rain.

16. An alternative to NEXRAD called _____ delivers to the flight crew weather information products, such as NEXRAD precipitation maps, METAR, NOTAMS, PIREPS and winds aloft data.

17. The radar altimeter was one of the first systems designed to help the flight crew avoid _____; although, they are not very accurate above about _____ AGL.

18. In contrast to radar altimeters, _____ take into consideration the phase of flight and the terrain forward of the aircraft.

19. The ability to look around the flight path of the aircraft is called _____.

20. Class B TAWS relies mostly on a position reported by the _____ and the _____.

21. The typical Class B TAWS issues a voice callout, "_____," when the aircraft nears the decision height.

22. EGPWS stands for _____ and satisfies requirements for _____.

23. Aircraft with an EGPWS often rely on a/an _____ to provide attitude and heading information, along with navigation, or a/an _____ to provide attitude and heading information (no navigation).

24. The EGPWS can monitor all the data bus inputs and the discrete inputs to determine the _____ and the _____.

25. Optimized for rotorcraft operation, Heli-TAWS is a class B TAWS whose database includes terrain and _____, that are hazardous to helicopters.

26. In a terrain display, colors represent terrain elevation as follows: more than 1,000 below the aircraft's elevation shows as _____; between 1,000 and 100 shows as _____; and at an elevation 100 below the aircraft or closer shows as _____.

27. Pilots should not rely too much on weather radar for _____ because weather radar beam width is too wide to detect hazardous structures such as radio towers.

Chapter 4
Weather and Terrain Awareness and Avoidance

MULTIPLE CHOICE QUESTIONS

name:

date:

1. NWS Weather Forecast Offices (WFO) prepare how many Terminal Aerodrome Forecasts (TAF) for how many airports, and for how long are these forecasts are valid?
   a. 100 forecasts, 650 airports, 36 hours
   b. 120 forecasts, 700 airports, 12 hours
   c. 123 forecasts, more than 700 airports, 24 or 30 hours
   d. 200 forecasts, more than 200 airports, 10 hours

2. Having good weather information is important for flying safely. The regulations at 14 CFR Part 119 require the certificated airlines and operators to use what?
   a. Flight Service Stations
   b. NEXRAD or SiriusXM weather services
   c. Flight Information Services–Broadcast (FIS-B)
   d. The aeronautical weather information systems as defined in the Operations Specifications that FAA issues to the certificate holder

3. Which of these is NOT a basic preflight briefing that is available to the pilot?
   a. Standard briefing
   b. Quick briefing
   c. Abbreviated briefing
   d. Outlook briefing

4. Why do airborne radar systems have limited ability to detect dry snow, light snow, and water vapor?
   a. Those types of weather systems are too dry to reflect RF pulses.
   b. Those types of weather systems are too small.
   c. Those types of weather systems absorb too much of the RF pulses.
   d. Those types of weather systems scatter the RF pulse too much.

5. A "T," "W," or arrow appearing in the upper portion of a radar display indicates what?
   a. The radar system has detected traffic above the aircraft elevation.
   b. The radar system has detected activity beyond the range being displayed.
   c. A ground-based radar system is sending a message to the aircraft.
   d. ATC is sending a message to the aircraft.

6. Which of these best describes a rain gradient?
   a. The rain's density from the bottom of the storm system to the top
   b. The storm's wetness rating on the Reinold scale
   c. The distance between an area of no rain and an area of heavy rain
   d. The density of rain on a scale of 1 to 10

7. What feature do some radar systems provide that shows a storm in profile, thus helping flight crews visualize at what altitudes most of the precipitation is falling?
   a. Horizontal view scan
   b. Density scan
   c. Vertical scan
   d. Side scan

8. When is a predictive wind shear system active?
   a. Any time the radar altimeter is active
   b. Any time the aircraft is flying
   c. Only when the aircraft is between 50 and 1,000 ft. AGL
   d. Only when the aircraft is in landing configuration

9. Why is the Ryan LFWM system able to show the location of turbulence where a standard radar system cannot?
   a. It detects where any precipitation is occurring, even if it is a dry type of precipitation (e.g., light snow).
   b. It plots turbulence using Doppler radar.
   c. It plots where electrical discharges are occurring, which are often caused by wind shear in storms.
   d. It detects the steepest area of a rain gradient, where it is usually most turbulent.

10. In an LFWM system, because current induced from a lightning strike at 0° creates an identical signature to one at 180° and the signature at 90° is identical to that at 270°, this creates what, which a loop antenna alone is not sufficient to resolve?
    a. Profile uncertainty
    b. Ambiguity
    c. Confusion
    d. Azimuth uncertainty

Chapter 4
Weather and Terrain Awareness and Avoidance

MULTIPLE CHOICE QUESTIONS

name:

date:

11. To receive and use SiriusXM weather, the aircraft owner or operator must have what, in addition to a satellite receiver with antenna and a display?
    a. An FAA-approved certificate
    b. A NEXRAD account
    c. A subscription to SiriusXM
    d. All the above

12. Which of these is NOT an advantage that NEXRAD has over airborne radar systems?
    a. It provides real-time weather information.
    b. It can detect the types of weather that airborne radar cannot.
    c. It can detect weather beyond an airborne radar system's range.
    d. It can be received by several modes.

13. What is the maximum range of a NEXRAD transmitter station?
    a. 150 NM
    b. 500 NM
    c. 250 NM
    d. 220 NM

14. Aircraft flying under different FAR parts have different TAWS requirements. Which FAR parts and TAWS requirements match up?
    a. Part 91 = Class B TAWS; Part 121 = Class A TAWS; Part 135 = Class A or B TAWS depending on aircraft age and number of seats
    b. Part 91 = Class A TAWS; Part 121 = Class A TAWS; Part 135 = Class B TAWS
    c. Part 91 = Class B TAWS; Part 121 = Class B TAWS; Part 135 = Class A or B TAWS depending on aircraft age and number of seats
    d. Part 91 = Class A TAWS; Part 121 = Class A TAWS; Part 135 = Class A or B TAWS depending on company certificate

15. At minimum, Class B TAWS must provide the flight crew which three indications?
    a. Excessive Rate of Descent—Mode 1, Excessive Closure Rate—Mode 2, and Negative Climb Rate or Altitude Loss after Takeoff—Mode 3
    b. Excessive Rate of Descent—Mode 1, Negative Climb Rate or Altitude Loss after Takeoff—Mode 3, and Altitude Callouts and Excessive Bank Angle Alert—Mode 6
    c. Excessive Rate of Descent—Mode 1, Significant Descent below the ILS Landing Glide Path—Mode 5, and Altitude Callouts and Excessive Bank Angle Alert—Mode 6
    d. Excessive Rate of Descent—Mode 1, Negative Climb Rate or Altitude Loss after Takeoff—Mode 3, and Significant Descent below the ILS Landing Glide Path—Mode 5

16. EGPWS receives information from the navigation, instrument, and maintenance systems via what, and it receives information from the aircraft, such as angle of attack, landing gear position, and flap position, which are categorized as what?
    a. Data network, discrete inputs
    b. Local area network, binary inputs
    c. Data bus, discrete inputs and outputs
    d. Secure wifi, coaxial cable inputs

17. The air data system uses air data modules that do what and then supply the data to the what, which processes the information and supplies it to the data bus?
    a. Process static pressure information, data coaxial unit
    b. Sample pitot/static pressure information, air data combination unit
    c. Convert air pressure information to analog format, ADIRU
    d. Digitize air pressure information, air data computer

18. A terrain display usually relies on what to compare the position and altitude of the aircraft against the terrain data from an internal topographical database?
    a. A GNSS location signal
    b. ADS-B transponder
    c. Radar altimeter
    d. Radar system in ground map mode

19. When performing an operational test on an EGPWS, which of the following is not part of the preparation?
    a. The flaps must be operated; be sure that the flaps area is clear of personnel and equipment.
    b. The landing gear must be down, locked, pins installed, and the power removed from the landing gear system.
    c. The IRS must be energized and properly aligned.
    d. The mode 2 warnings—involving altitude change, radar altitude, and airspeed data—are active.

Chapter 4
Weather and Terrain Awareness and Avoidance

ANALYSIS QUESTIONS

name:

date:

1. When would a pilot receive an abbreviated weather briefing?

2. What symptoms could occur as a result of antenna stabilization failure?

3. Why do ground targets look distorted on the radar screen?

4. When the airborne radar display shows an area of intense precipitation at a range of 30 NM, a gap, and another area of medium-level precipitation behind the first at 70 NM, what should the pilot assume?

5. Just after installation, an LFWM system displays weather to the left of the aircraft on the right side of the display. What problem could cause this?

6. An LFWM shows lightning activity consistently ahead of the aircraft at a distance of 20 NM, even though no storms are in the area. How would you troubleshoot this problem?

Chapter 4
Weather and Terrain Awareness and Avoidance

ANALYSIS QUESTIONS

name:

date:

7. Why should a pilot avoid using NEXRAD provided by the SiriusXM system to weave around severe weather?

8. Why are radar altimeters not useful above 2,000 ft. AGL?

9. How are TAWS able to look forward for terrain avoidance?

10. How will an inoperative GNSS receiver affect the TAWS B?

11. What are the limitations of using weather radar for terrain avoidance?

Chapter 5
Synthetic and Enhanced Vision

FILL IN THE BLANK QUESTIONS

name:

date:

1. An SVS gathers input from multiple aircraft components and systems and displays a/an _____ version of the outside world.

2. An SVS shows its information on a/an _____, which is directly in the pilot's view out the windshield, or on a/an _____, such as an EADI.

3. Two types of views an SVS displays are exocentric (seen from _____ point of view) and egocentric (seen from _____ point of view).

4. List at least four data inputs that an SVS uses to create its version of the outside world. _____

5. SVS terrain display shows topography with an array of colors and shades to differentiate the _____ of surrounding terrain to achieve a 3D effect.

6. An SVS shows human-built objects that are a threat; a feature that is called _____.

7. An SVS represents a flight path as a series of _____.

8. Most SVS data inputs are transmitted to the SVS processor via _____.

9. In an SVS installation that was not planned well enough, if the already installed systems are incompatible, they must be _____, greatly increasing cost and time to complete the installation.

10. Most SVS installation manuals have _____, which help you plan out which channels are used for which required parameters.

11. An EVS provides _____ of what is ahead in the aircraft's path, even in conditions preventing the flight crew from seeing.

12. FLIR cameras sense energy from the _____ of the electromagnetic spectrum, allowing them to sense _____, which can be processed to generate images.

13. The best-performing IR sensors in an EVS require cooling to _____ to produce images in misty and foggy conditions.

14. If an EVS requires cooling, the time it takes from startup to image display can be _____.

15. EVS are not to be used for _____; they are approved for situational awareness only.

Chapter 5
Synthetic and Enhanced Vision

FILL IN THE BLANK QUESTIONS

name:

date:

16. Flight crews, especially in _____ , use night vision goggles, which are a specialized EVS.

17. NVG external light source requirements range in generations from _____ needing the most light to _____ needing the least.

18. Before they may use NVG, flight crews must complete ground and flight _____ for NVG, and the flight crews must _____ .

19. For an EFVS, name at least four aircraft information types or attributes that are displayed with the thermal image. _____ _____

20. Combined vision systems consist of both _____ and _____ technology combined in a single image.

21. In the future, CVS could allow for operation in _____ in civil aviation.

Chapter 5
Synthetic and Enhanced Vision

MULTIPLE CHOICE QUESTIONS

name:

date:

1. SVS and EVS improve aviation safety because flight crews are more aware of what?
   a. Exact timing until the aircraft's landing
   b. Aircraft position in relation to terrain and obstacles in reduced visual conditions
   c. Weather conditions ahead
   d. Aircraft position in relation to the runway

2. Which of the following is not something that an SVS can display?
   a. Terrain
   b. Obstacles
   c. Weather systems to avoid
   d. Projected flight path with the corridor or box display

3. What is the major difference between SVS head up and head down displays?
   a. Head up displays use three colors, and head down are full color
   b. Head up displays are full color, and head down are monochrome
   c. Head up displays are monochrome, and head down are full color
   d. Both are full color, but the head up displays are lower resolution

4. Removing an obstacle from an SVS display, if it poses no threat to the aircraft, is a task that is called what?
   a. Decluttering the display
   b. Delisting the display
   c. Simplifying the display
   d. Rasterizing the display

5. If terrain infringes on an aircraft's projected flight path, the SVS displays it as yellow or red using which distances below the aircraft?
   a. Yellow if it is between 50 and 500 ft. below; red if it is closer than 50 ft., ranging to higher than the aircraft
   b. Yellow if it is between 150 and 1,500 ft. below; red if it is closer than 150 ft., ranging to higher than the aircraft
   c. Yellow if it is between 200 and 1,200 ft. below; red if it is closer than 200 ft., ranging to higher than the aircraft
   d. Yellow if it is between 100 and 1,000 ft. below; red if it is closer than 100 ft., ranging to higher than the aircraft

6. Which of the following is something that flight crews are not allowed to use SVS to do?
   a. Gain situational awareness
   b. Navigate
   c. View a 3D representation of obstacles
   d. Avoid terrain

7. Messages sent on an ARINC 429 bus consist of bit words that are how long and of these, how many bits are for labeling and how many are the information itself?
   a. 50 total; 8 bits for labeling; 42 bits for the information itself
   b. 48 total; 10 bits for labeling; 38 bits for the information itself
   c. 32 total; 8 bits for labeling; 24 bits for the information itself
   d. 24 total; 4 bits for labeling; 20 bits for the information itself

8. In an EVS, the technology used is called FLIR, which stands for what?
   a. Fixed length image reduction
   b. Fine luminous infrared radar
   c. Flux laminated image resolver
   d. Forward looking infrared

9. Of the three bands in the infrared spectrum when used in an EVS, which one requires an external light source to be detected?
   a. Long wave infrared (LWIR)
   b. Intermediate wave infrared (IWIR)
   c. Medium wave infrared (MWIR)
   d. Short wave infrared (SWIR)

10. In an EVS sensor, lenses focus the IR energy onto what so it can be changed to what and sent to the processor?
    a. Sensor pixel plate, electrical energy
    b. Charge coupled device, X and Y coordinates
    c. Liquid crystal sensor, magnetic pulses
    d. Refractometer, visible light

Chapter 5
Synthetic and Enhanced Vision

MULTIPLE CHOICE QUESTIONS

name:

date:

11. Because of export restrictions on EVS, the IR sensor must be difficult to remove. Some manufacturers design sensor units so that if it is removed from the aircraft, what happens?
    a. It explodes
    b. It becomes unusable or is destroyed
    c. It releases toxic dye
    d. It transmits the unit's location coordinates to a satellite receiver so it can be found

12. In night vision goggle's internal components, a microchannel plate receives electrons and amplifies and directs them toward what other component, which then releases and sends photons to the next component.
    a. Objective lens
    b. Eyepiece lens
    c. Phosphor screen
    d. Photocathode

13. Why must flight deck and external aircraft lighting be modified to work with NVG?
    a. So the lights are all the same color
    b. So the lighting does not interfere with the NVG
    c. So the lights are all the same brightness
    d. So the lighting is all NVIS red

14. What is the main difference between EFVS and EVS?
    a. EFVS are less expensive
    b. EVS are simpler to maintain
    c. EFVS have added primary flight display information to the display
    d. All the above

15. Why are some advanced vision systems not capable of sensing light emitting diode (LED) lights, compared to incandescent lights?
    a. The LEDs have different wavelength and are cooler
    b. The LEDs are not as bright
    c. The LEDs are blueish and not as easily detectable
    d. The LEDs do not emit as many photons

Chapter 5
Synthetic and Enhanced Vision

ANALYSIS QUESTIONS

name:

date:

1. After landing, the SVS warnings are still displayed/annunciated. What could cause this?

2. Flight path indications are not appearing on the SVS display. What are the possible causes?

3. A new SVS is installed in an aircraft, and the SVS processor ARINC 429 data bus does not communicate with the Attitude Heading and Reference System. Configurations are checked and found to be correct. What are the possible causes?

4. A failed SVS processor was replaced. When the new one is powered up, you find that no data is being processed or displayed correctly. What should you check first

5. Ice is building up on the EVS sensor window. What are the possible causes?

6. Failure warnings appear on the EVS display and video is inhibited. What should be done?

Chapter 5
Synthetic and Enhanced Vision

ANALYSIS QUESTIONS

name:

date:

7. What EVS maintenance is required?

8. Instrument lights are overpowering the image displayed on the NVG. What's the solution?

9. The IR camera displayed on the HUD is not aligned properly. What is the solution?

Chapter 6
Avionics Bench Equipment and Practices

FILL IN THE BLANK QUESTIONS

name:

date:

1. Older avionics units used to have analog transistors; many now use _____ _____. Repair shops tend to replace _____ in a unit because doing so is less costly than troubleshooting and fixing them.

2. Understanding a system and its units and how they all work helps you determine what is wrong with the system. Name four of the many tools or resources you can use to analyze a system: _____ _____

3. After analyzing the problem in a system, the second step in troubleshooting is to _____, which you usually begin by visually inspecting the unit.

4. Broken wiring, loose terminal or plug connections, faulty relays, and faulty switches are all _____ that interrupt power through a circuit.

5. The _____ is useful for finding opens, shorts, grounds, or incorrect resistance values.

6. Even if you cannot check mechanical linkages, mounting assemblies, switch actuators, and similar equipment with a volt-ohmmeter, the three basic rules for troubleshooting remain the same: _____ .

7. The MM is a good resource to check when fixing a problem; it lists _____ you need and describes _____ to a system unit or area.

8. Never use _____ as a method of troubleshooting.

9. When removing an old part and installing the new one, if you cannot finish the job immediately, you should _____ from the aircraft until you can finish the job.

10. Use procedures and specialized test sets to perform tests on units when _____ _____ .

11. If an avionics unit has an intermittent problem, it can help to find the problem by changing the unit's temperature, such as by _____ overnight or for a few hours, and then powering it up and testing it.

12. Because technical capabilities are advancing all the time, you must stay current by being _____ .

13. When you are troubleshooting a unit and it is taking a long time to discover the problem, the cost to fix it can quickly surpass the cost of _____ _____ .

Chapter 6
Avionics Bench Equipment and Practices

FILL IN THE BLANK QUESTIONS

name:

date:

14. Before you touch a sensitive unit, put on _____.

15. When hooking up a test meter, select the _____ range first, and then switch to _____ ranges as needed.

16. A multimeter is a versatile tool that can measure _____ _____.

17. Most avionics units have a/an _____ that receives the power from the aircraft or bench power supply and divides it and distributes it to other internal units requiring other voltages and amounts.

18. A navigation receiver test set simulates flying in a set direction or heading and see if the _____ unit is operating properly.

19. The navigation receiver test set checks the frequency response simulating an approach so that the _____ come on.

20. ADF, which stands for _____, technology is being replaced by _____. Consequently, the ADF test set might not be used much.

21. An autopilot test set, when used to troubleshoot a flight control system, is placed in series with the harnesses of the two aircraft _____ and several _____.

22. A/An _____ is used to check capacitors for value and for _____ at the rated working voltage on a digital readout, and to check inductors for inductance and for quality.

23. To test a radar system, use a radar test set that simulates _____ an aircraft might detect.

24. A/An _____ is used to test the power supply for units requiring unique power in the aircraft. This is useful for testing that units, such as the RMI and navigation units or gyroscopes, are receiving the _____.

25. _____ is a method of determining where in a circuit a discontinuity is.

26. TDR, which stands for _____, is a measurement technology widely used for analyzing _____ and finding faults, such as in wiring.

Chapter 6
Avionics Bench Equipment and Practices

MULTIPLE CHOICE QUESTIONS

name:

date:

1. Troubleshooting jobs become simple by breaking it down into steps. Which of these is NOT one of the steps?
    a. Detect and isolate the trouble
    b. Analyze the symptom
    c. Order the replacement unit
    d. Correct the trouble and test the work

2. When detecting a problem, if a circuit breaker has opened, reset or replace it and apply power. If it opens again, what should you do?
    a. Secure the power because the circuit likely has a malfunction, and do not apply power until you have corrected the malfunction.
    b. Reset it once more, and apply power.
    c. Remove the unit and take readings with a voltmeter.
    d. Reset it at least two more times; a total of three is required before you remove the unit.

3. When the problem is hard to determine, it might be helpful to do what to a unit, such as when it is functioning but does not measure up to minimum standards?
    a. Apply double the power it requires
    b. Conduct bench tests
    c. Conduct ohmmeter tests
    d. Conduct voltmeter circuit tests

4. When fixing a problem and you must leave power cables exposed, which of the following should you do?
    a. Prevent them from shorting out by using an insulating cover.
    b. Place a warning sign on the main power switch in the flight deck and on the external power receptacle.
    c. Disconnect the aircraft battery.
    d. All the above

5. Small items lost in an aircraft present what type of hazard, which can down an aircraft?
    a. Foreign object damage (FOD)
    b. Minimal-sized asset damage (MSAD)
    c. Radio frequency interference (RFI)
    d. All the above

6. The final step of a troubleshooting job or fix is to do what?
    a. Perform a unit test on the bench, then install the unit in the aircraft.
    b. Install the unit in the aircraft.
    c. Install the unit and test the equipment and confirm that it is fixed and operating correctly
    d. Turn on the unit and make sure it powers up properly.

7. When searching for a trouble spot in a unit, what is an effective way to inspect it?
    a. Look for burn marks and smell for burns
    b. Blow it off with high-pressure air
    c. Hold it up to a bright light to inspect for holes in the unit that allow light through
    d. Apply power to see if it sparks

8. After a unit is fixed, what is the best reason for performing a final and complete check on the bench and again once it is installed in the aircraft?
    a. To make sure it powers up okay
    b. To verify that all is working
    c. Your boss probably requires it
    d. It is not necessary to test the unit again in the aircraft if it works on the bench

9. As part of an avionics technician's career best practices, what are some good ways to build up your own library of resources?
    a. Collect material that helped you understand electronics or avionics concepts
    b. Keep articles or other training materials from classes or training you attended
    c. Keep a list of, or bookmark, the websites that are useful
    d. All the above

10. If you are interrupted in performing a procedure, note where you left off. When you resume, what should you do?
    a. Go back a step or two and proceed from there
    b. Start over at the beginning
    c. Go back at least three steps
    d. Start right where you left off

Chapter 6
Avionics Bench Equipment and Practices

MULTIPLE CHOICE QUESTIONS

name:

date:

11. Which are not some of the basic components used in schematic diagrams?
    a. Transistor, inductor
    b. Diode, transformer, resistor
    c. Integrated circuit, capacitor
    d. Wire, power supply

12. Why should you never measure the resistance of a meter or a circuit with a meter in it?
    a. The high current required to measure the meter can cause a fire.
    b. You could be shocked.
    c. The high current required to measure the meter can damage the meter.
    d. The high current required to measure the meter can melt the wires.

13. Which of the following is not a type of power the aircraft typically supplies to avionics units?
    a. 220 volt, 200 Hz AC
    b. 14 volt DC
    c. 28 volt DC
    d. 26 volt, 400 Hz AC

14. Which of the following is an example of what an air traffic control transponder test set can test?
    a. Check the course deviation indicator pointer deflection accuracy.
    b. Measure receiver bandwidth and minimum threshold level (MTL)
    c. Perform standard tests on aircraft audio controller and amplifier panels
    d. All the above

15. A navigation receiver test set can be used to perform many tests. Which of these is not one?
    a. Check that the unit's bearing accuracy is within manufacturer's specifications
    b. Check standard centering accuracy or error limits of the unit.
    c. Check the gain of all antennas and meets FAA standards
    d. Check that the glideslope deviation pointer is centered

16. A communications transmitter test set is primarily used to test whether a communications unit transceiver is broadcasting a signal correctly. Many units can also perform which of the following?
    a. Function as a duplex generator, a modulation meter, oscilloscope, spectrum analyzer, modulation meter, and a SINAD distortion meter
    b. Monitor AM, FM, and single side band signals
    c. Generate RF signals
    d. All the above

17. What type of test set can simulate the functions and controls as if the aircraft is flying at a set height above ground level or reaching a decision height?
    a. Automatic direction finder test set
    b. Radar altimeter test set
    c. Course deviation indicator test set
    d. NAV/COMM test set

18. Which test set is used to calibrate both manual and automatic VOR converters, the VOR section of area navigation (RNAV) units, and, when used in conjunction with a control/interface panel, monitor the deviation and flag current outputs?
    a. Universal heading and track selector test set
    b. Radar and spectrum analyzer test set
    c. Course deviation indicator test set
    d. Air traffic control transponder test set

19. In addition to testing capacitors and inductors, you can use the capacitor and inductor analyzer to conduct other tests such as what?
    a. To test whether switches, PC boards, connectors, and so on are working
    b. To find the resistance value of a circuit
    c. To find the distance to opens or a short in a transmission line
    d. To find the ohms of resistance in a speaker system

20. To use a radar and spectrum analyzer test set, connect the radar unit with a coaxial cable to what?
    a. A waveguide termination (dummy load)
    b. A waveguide coupler and a waveguide termination (dummy load)
    c. The antenna in the radome
    d. The radar transceiver unit

Chapter 6
Avionics Bench Equipment and Practices

MULTIPLE CHOICE QUESTIONS

name:

date:

21. Signal generators are test units that you can use to send a signal to a unit to verify an alignment signal. To do this, you could perform which of the following, as one example?
    a. Send to a microphone an amplitude signal as specified in the MM and check that the result matches the MM-specified value
    b. Send to the communications unit transceiver a signal that is outside the unit's detection range and check that the unit registers it as such
    c. Attach a coaxial cable to the VOR receiver and see if it returns the correct heading value
    d. Send an amplitude signal to the radar altimeter antenna cable

22. Using a time domain reflectometer, you can find the distance to a discontinuity in a coaxial cable by measuring what?
    a. The difference of the frequency in the transmitted pulse and the reflected pulse
    b. The frequency of the reflected pulse
    c. The amplitude of the reflected pulse
    d. The time required for the pulse to travel to the discontinuity and back

Chapter 6
Avionics Bench Equipment and Practices

ANALYSIS QUESTIONS

name:

date:

1. An avionics unit is reported as faulty. As you attempt to verify this, sometimes the unit works; sometimes not. How should you proceed?

2. After a unit is fixed, installed, and tested to work properly, the unit still is not officially ready to return to service; therefore, the aircraft may not fly. Why not?

3. Using the troubleshooting chart here for a transponder, what should you do if the transponder is not reporting the altitude correctly?

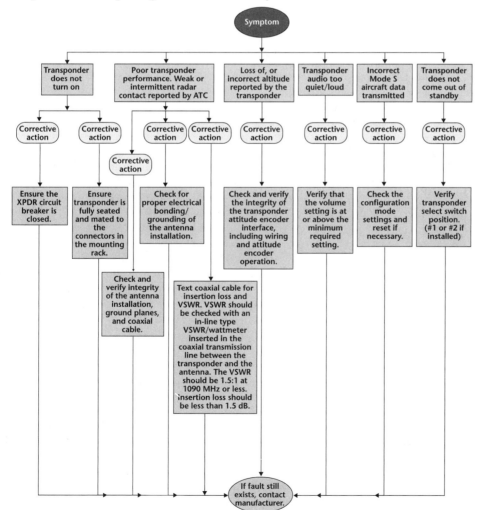

Chapter 6
Avionics Bench Equipment and Practices

ANALYSIS QUESTIONS

name:

date:

4. You are working on an avionics unit and determine that the unit itself is not working properly. Explain some techniques for localizing the faulty part in the unit.

5. Why is it important to know the value of an avionics unit and how much a customer is being charged for your work to troubleshoot and fix it?

6. Using the following schematic determine how many transistors and how many diodes are used in this inverter.

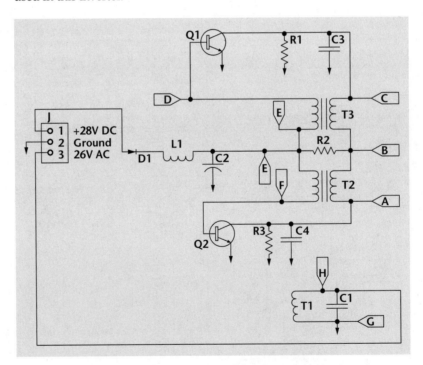

7. Referring to the schematic shown in the previous question, what would be the reading on a voltmeter connected between point G and ground?

Chapter 7
Emergency-Related Avionics

FILL IN THE BLANK QUESTIONS

name:

date:

1. When sufficient power is not being produced for everything, aircraft use a process called _____, which turns off nonessential loads, leaving more power for essential loads.

2. After an APU engine reaches its operating r.p.m., it can be used for _____ and for _____.

3. A device called the _____, when deployed by opening a door in the fuselage, operates a hydraulic pump, a generator, or both in combination to provide power when the primary sources are lost.

4. Any change of battery type in an aircraft is considered a/an _____.

5. Large transport aircraft generally use _____ or _____ types of batteries.

6. For a NiCd battery, a combination of high battery temperature (higher than _____) and overcharging can lead to a condition called _____.

7. Many aircraft are required to have two recorders onboard: a cockpit voice recorder and a flight data recorder, which are called _____.

8. Old flight data recorders record data on _____; new ones record data on _____.

9. Before data is recorded in a flight data recorder, modern aircraft use _____ to receive information from multiple places, format the data, then send it to the data recorder.

10. The cockpit voice recorder is usually mounted in the _____ where it is more likely to remain intact in a crash.

11. In addition to recording on flight data recorders, some aircraft in service for large airlines are _____ in real-time or in regular bursts from the aircraft to data storage servers via _____.

12. An ELT, which stands for _____, is a device that helps search parties find downed aircraft.

13. The digital ELTs permit the COSPAS-SARSAT satellite system to narrow the search area to a relatively small area—within about _____.

14. Unlike with digital ELT alerts, search and rescue teams' normal practice is to wait for a confirmation of an analog ELT alert by a/an _____ or similar notification—all in an effort to avoid _____.

Chapter 7
Emergency-Related Avionics

FILL IN THE BLANK QUESTIONS

name:

date:

15. The ELT antenna should be as far aft on the aircraft as practicable and _____ _____ from other VHF antennas to prevent interference.

16. ELT batteries must be able to power the ELT for _____ hours.

17. If you are testing an analog ELT, the time to test is limited to the _____ _____ of any hour.

Chapter 7
Emergency-Related Avionics

MULTIPLE CHOICE QUESTIONS

name:

date:

1. In order of regular operation to emergency operation, aircraft power is supplied by what items?
   a. Engine-driven DC generators, batteries, APU-driven DC generators
   b. Engine-driven AC generators, APU-driven AC generators, RAT, batteries
   c. Engine-driven AC generators, RAT, APU-driven AC generators, batteries
   d. Engine-driven DC generators, batteries, APU-driven DC generators

2. Which of these best describes how aircraft main batteries are used?
   a. Many functions: ground power, emergency power, improving DC bus stability, and fault clearing
   b. Only a few functions: emergency power and fault clearing
   c. Only a few functions: ground power, emergency power, flight data recorders, ELTs
   d. A few functions: ground power, improving DC bus stability, cockpit voice recorders, flight data recorders, ELTs

3. Which types of batteries are used in general aviation and turbine powered aircraft and are sometimes authorized replacements for NiCd batteries?
   a. Lithium ion
   b. Lead phosphorus
   c. Nickel-potassium
   d. Valve-regulated lead-acid

4. Which battery type may use a flammable electrolyte?
   a. Nickel-cadmium
   b. Valve-regulated lead-acid
   c. Lithium ion
   d. Lead-acid

5. Which of these is not a correct survivability standard for data and voice recorders?
   a. High-intensity fire of 2,012°F for 30 minutes
   b. Sea water immersion for 30 days
   c. Low-intensity fire 600°F for 24 hours
   d. Impact shock of 3,400 Gs for 6.5 milliseconds

6. Although a flight data recorder's digital media, such as an array of memory boards, can record up to several hundred parameters, how many are required as a minimum on new aircraft?
   a. 102
   b. 95
   c. 90
   d. 88

7. The ULB, or *pinger*, helps crash investigators locate the flight data recorder under water. What activates the pinger, and to what depth can it still transmit?
   a. The recorder is immersed in water, 14,000 ft.
   b. The force on it exceeds 50 Gs, 12,000 ft.
   c. The force on it exceeded 50 Gs and it is immersed in water, 20,000 ft.
   d. The flight crew switches it on, 15,000 ft.

8. Early voice recorders that use magnetic tape could record for how long before recording over previously recorded sounds?
   a. 2 hours
   b. 1 hour
   c. 30 minutes
   d. 45 minutes

9. Newer digital voice recorders must record a minimum of how long before recording over previous recordings?
   a. 1 hour
   b. 2 hours
   c. 3 hours
   d. 1.5 hours

10. Which of these is not an appropriate use or treatment of the data recorded by video recorders?
    a. Kept secure
    b. Used for investigating an accident or improving operations
    c. Used as a basis for personnel termination
    d. Released only under permission from management

Chapter 7
Emergency-Related Avionics

MULTIPLE CHOICE QUESTIONS

name:

date:

11. The general aviation analog ELT operates at what MHz, and the newer digital ELT operates at what MHz?
    a. 121.5 and 243.0
    b. 243 and 401.5
    c. 123 and 243.5
    d. 121.5 and 406

12. What system, if used with a new digital ELT, can lead search parties to within 100 yards of a crash location because it provides accurate information that the ELT sends as part of the initial alert?
    a. A 121.5-MHz transmitter
    b. Air traffic control radar beacon system (ATCRBS)
    c. Global positioning system (GPS)
    d. Electronic flight instrument system (EFIS)

13. ELTs must be mounted securely in the aircraft. Because of this, hook and loop fasteners are not the best way to fasten the ELT to the aircraft—unless what?
    a. They are supplemented with a front mounting bracket
    b. They are certified by the manufacturer
    c. They are inspected by and approved by the FAA
    d. They are reported on a form 830

14. What is the preferred way to test an ELT to prevent broadcasting signals that could trigger a false alert?
    a. In a shielded or screened room or a test container designed for testing ELTs
    b. By removing the antenna and replacing it with a dummy load
    c. In a closed hangar
    d. Pressing the self-test button

15. Because ELTs can activate as a result of aerobatics, hard landings, movement by ground crews and aircraft maintenance, what should you do as a final step after performing maintenance on an ELT?
    a. Disconnect it and reconnect it
    b. Replace the battery
    c. Use the self-test feature
    d. Verify that the ELT is not transmitting

Chapter 7
Emergency-Related Avionics

ANALYSIS QUESTIONS

name:

date:

1. Explain what an APU is and its uses in aircraft.

2. You are asked to service the battery on an aircraft. When you locate it, you find a battery with six large caps on the top. What type of battery is this, what is the operating voltage, and what is the most common service needed?

3. What similarities do NiCd and Li-ion batteries have?

4. List at least three survivability standards that flight data and voice recorders must meet.

Chapter 7
Emergency-Related Avionics

ANALYSIS QUESTIONS

name:

date:

5. Describe how modern flight data recorders acquire and record data.

6. What benefits do digital ELTs have over analog ELTs?

7. After inspecting an ELT, replacing its battery, running the built-in test, and reinstalling it, what is the next thing you should do? Explain how to do it and why.